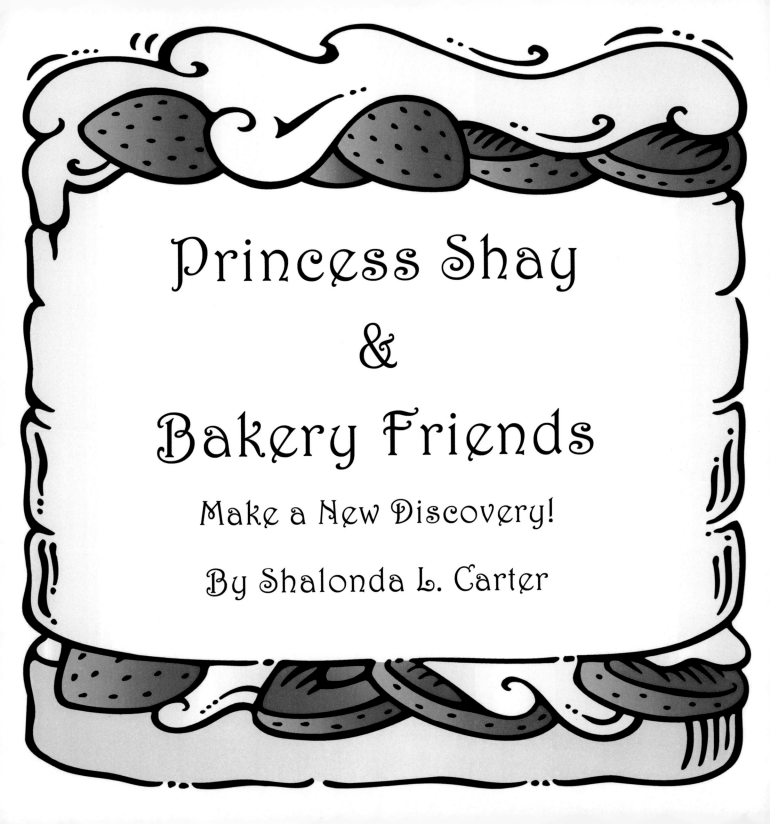

Princess Shay

&

Bakery Friends

Make a New Discovery!

By Shalonda L. Carter

AuthorHouse™ LLC
1663 Liberty Drive
Bloomington, IN 47403
www.authorhouse.com
Phone: 1-800-839-8640

Published by AuthorHouse 09/19/2014

ISBN: 978-1-4520-0702-1 (sc)

Library of Congress Control Number: 2011906496

Any people depicted in stock imagery provided by Thinkstock are models,
and such images are being used for illustrative purposes only.
Certain stock imagery © Thinkstock.

This book is printed on acid-free paper.

THIS BOOK BELONGS TO:

_____

(Name)

Dedication

Mary E. Carter
"Ethel Mae Jordan"
Happy 80th Birthday!

This book is dedicated to the loving memory of my grandmother. She was my culinary mentor who possessed more than thirty years of occupational experience as a cook in the Mississippi Public School District's cafeteria. I believe she was right: "With God, all things are possible!"

Princess Shay loves to bake, and she does it quite well! She makes cookies, brownies, even pies, but most of all, she is known for her cakes.

Princess Shay

E veryone loves Princess Shay for her moist, delicious, and fabulous-looking cakes.

She bakes cakes for everyone with love truly from her heart, we say. "And who are we?" you may ask.

Allow us to introduce ourselves. We are Butter, Eggs, Sugar, Salt, Flour, and Vanilla! We are all the ingredients Princess Shay uses to bake.

Eggs

It's here the story begins as we tell you what happened one day when Princess Shay was done baking and left the kitchen for the day.

In a bold voice from the kitchen counter, Sugar spoke. "Princess Shay is gone for the day, so let's rest. Tomorrow, we will do our daily routine again with her in baking cookies, brownies, pies, and, of course, cakes!"

From the shelf above, Vanilla chimed in to exclaim, "That's right! We want to be at our best performance for our friend."

*A*ll the ingredients spoke at once, and others gave a nod in agreement.

*T*hen, from among the chatter, arose a shuffle… it was coming from the refrigerator! It was Little Brother Egg, the youngest of three siblings. In a soft, shy voice, he said, "Princess Shay is preparing to enter this year's Kingdom Cake Challenge, and I wonder who will be deemed the pastry world's most valuable ingredient to win the crowning title, Best Ingredient of the Year?"

Little Brother Egg

*T*here were more sounds of chatter and commotion all around the kitchen.

"Hear ye, hear ye!" Measuring Spoon (standing at attention) announced. "Shall we begin the official meeting of the ingredients?"

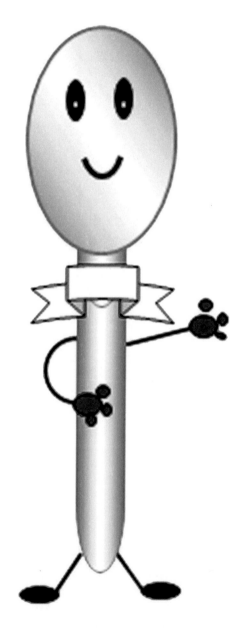

Measuring Spoon

Well, Little Butter, who was lying on his bed in the refrigerator, leaped to his feet and said, "I am smooth and creamy. Look at my beautiful golden-toned skin. I make each recipe truly decadent. I am sure to win!"

"Oh no! I am sorry, but it's the Eggs that hold all the recipes together. We are like the glue to bind everything together!" Big Brother Egg exclaimed as he took center stage in the refrigerator from his Little Brother Egg and Little Butter.

Big Brother Egg

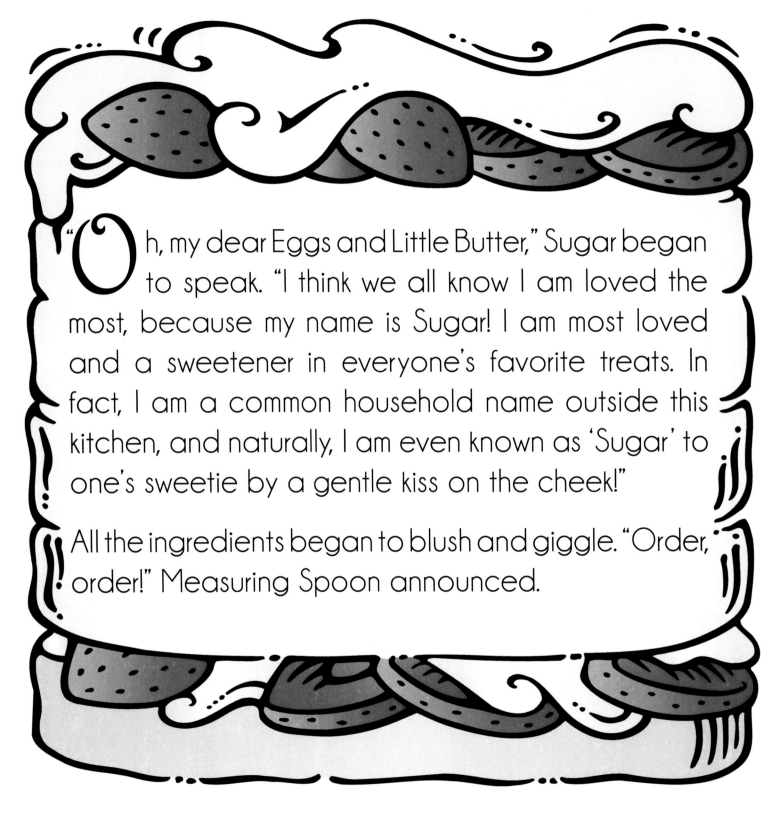

"Oh, my dear Eggs and Little Butter," Sugar began to speak. "I think we all know I am loved the most, because my name is Sugar! I am most loved and a sweetener in everyone's favorite treats. In fact, I am a common household name outside this kitchen, and naturally, I am even known as 'Sugar' to one's sweetie by a gentle kiss on the cheek!"

All the ingredients began to blush and giggle. "Order, order!" Measuring Spoon announced.

"Enough of all this!" Salt shouted.

All the ingredients remarked, "A little salty today, we see" as they started another round of giggles.

Salt replied, with a tone of assured attitude, "It's my salty flavor you will favor in contrast to sweet! Hmmm, sometimes, it's a welcomed compliment."

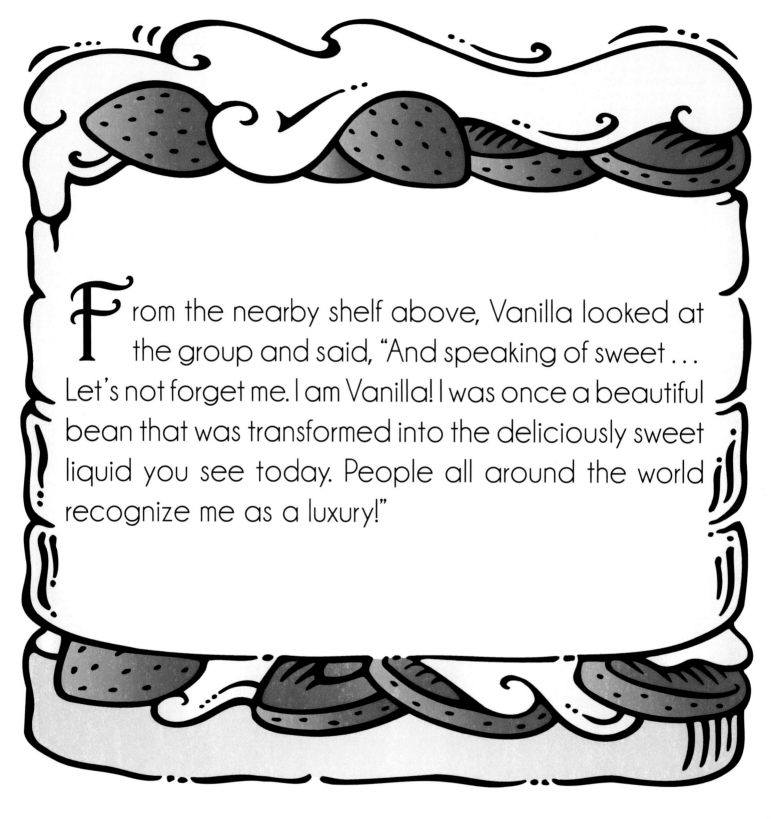

From the nearby shelf above, Vanilla looked at the group and said, "And speaking of sweet … Let's not forget me. I am Vanilla! I was once a beautiful bean that was transformed into the deliciously sweet liquid you see today. People all around the world recognize me as a luxury!"

Chatter once again filled the kitchen. While everyone was talking, Measuring Spoon reviewed the ingredient list to find no remarks had been recorded from Flour.

"Order, order, order in the kitchen!" shouted Measuring Spoon.

Then, on a shelf near the floor, Measuring Spoon looked down to see Flour and stated, "Why haven't you joined the meeting's conversation?"

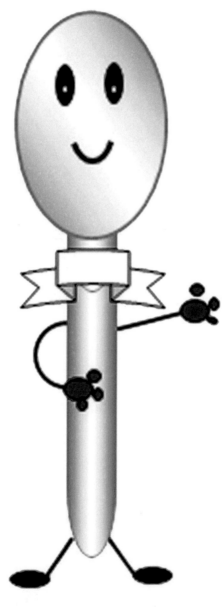

Measuring Spoon

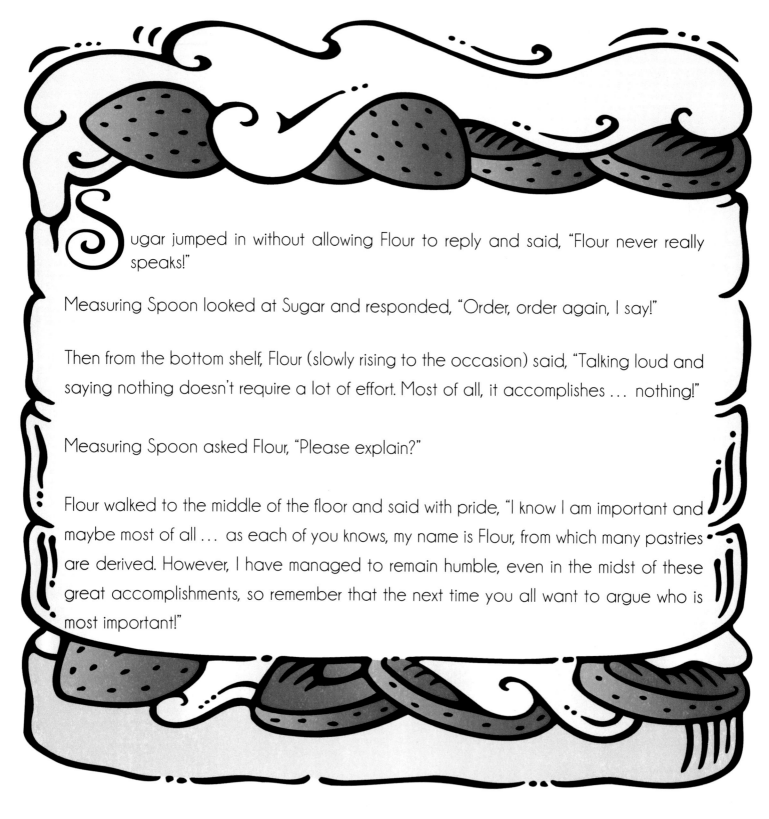

ugar jumped in without allowing Flour to reply and said, "Flour never really speaks!"

Measuring Spoon looked at Sugar and responded, "Order, order again, I say!"

Then from the bottom shelf, Flour (slowly rising to the occasion) said, "Talking loud and saying nothing doesn't require a lot of effort. Most of all, it accomplishes ... nothing!"

Measuring Spoon asked Flour, "Please explain?"

Flour walked to the middle of the floor and said with pride, "I know I am important and maybe most of all ... as each of you knows, my name is Flour, from which many pastries are derived. However, I have managed to remain humble, even in the midst of these great accomplishments, so remember that the next time you all want to argue who is most important!"

*T*he kitchen was now filled with silence as Flour spoke, because he often really didn't say a lot, but he always provided wisdom when he did stand up to speak.

All the ingredients looked at Flour and started to think for a moment, "Maybe Flour has a point ... Why fight and disagree when we all are important?"

Measuring Spoon prompted Flour, "Go ahead! You have the floor, and you may continue to speak."

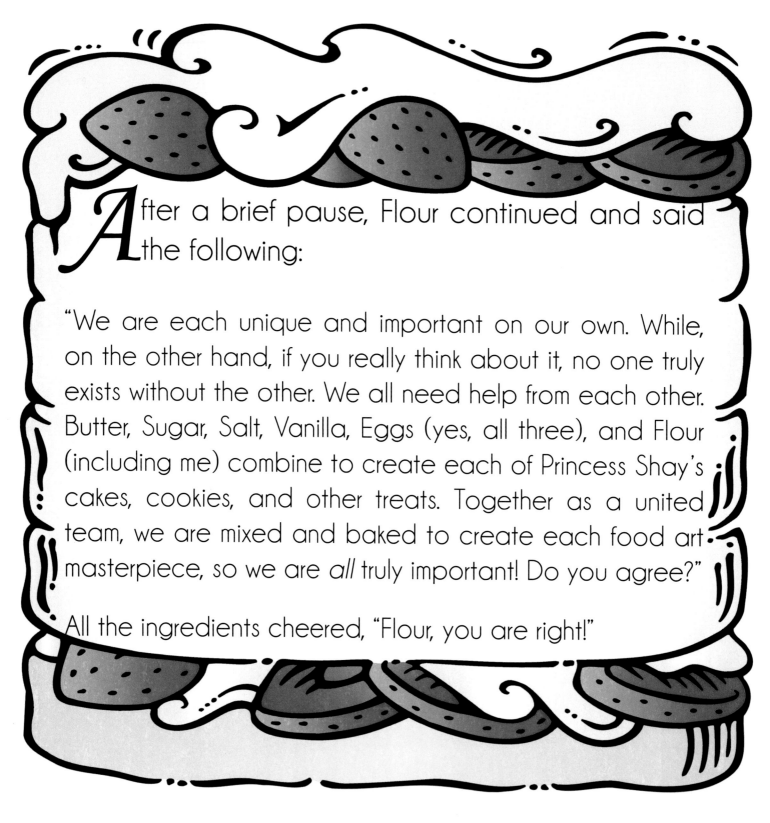

*A*fter a brief pause, Flour continued and said the following:

"We are each unique and important on our own. While, on the other hand, if you really think about it, no one truly exists without the other. We all need help from each other. Butter, Sugar, Salt, Vanilla, Eggs (yes, all three), and Flour (including me) combine to create each of Princess Shay's cakes, cookies, and other treats. Together as a united team, we are mixed and baked to create each food art masterpiece, so we are *all* truly important! Do you agree?"

All the ingredients cheered, "Flour, you are right!"

It was at that moment, from the kitchen counter, Ms. Cake stood upright and proudly said, "Yes, Flour, you are right! I should know, as a little bit of each of you is inside of me. You should all be equally proud, because every one of you helped to create me!"

Ms. Cake

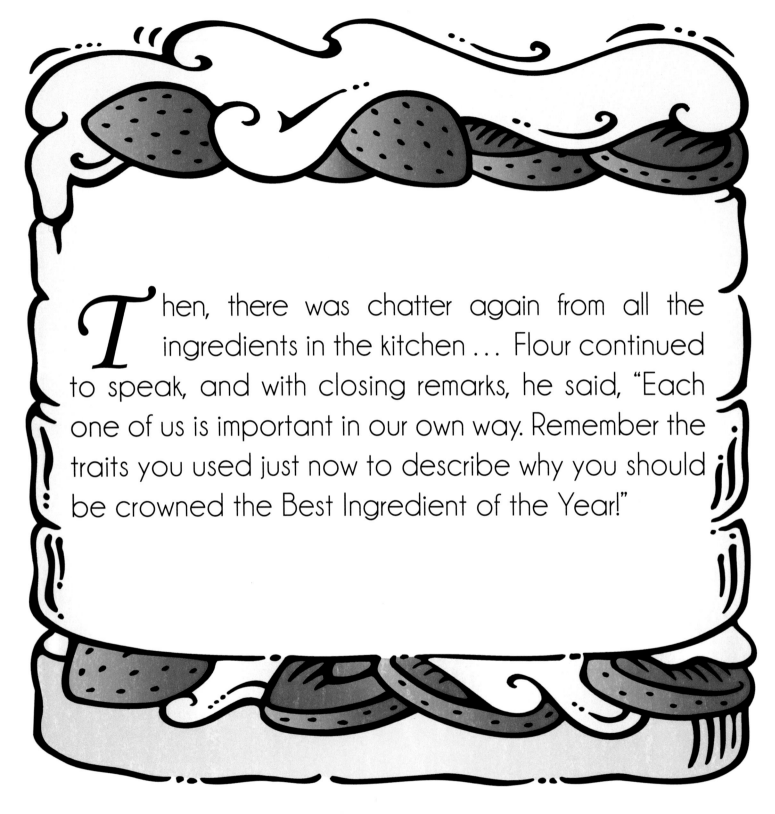

*T*hen, there was chatter again from all the ingredients in the kitchen … Flour continued to speak, and with closing remarks, he said, "Each one of us is important in our own way. Remember the traits you used just now to describe why you should be crowned the Best Ingredient of the Year!"

THE END

Until the next kitchen adventure …

A Letter from Princess Shay

Greetings Princes and Princesses all across the land,

Thank you for reading my story today! I would like to invite you to bake a cake with me. You will find all the tools and ingredients along with the recipe steps required on the next page. Meanwhile, if you don't have all the items, you can always use your favorite cake mix in the box to have some baking fun!

Don't forget to ask an adult family member for help.

If an adult family member does not have time to bake with us today, we can always use our imaginations. Cut out the stars of the story located in the book's activity section and pretend to mix them in the appropriate order to bake a beautiful cake. Please don't forget to ask an adult for help using the scissors.

Overall, I hope you had fun and learned a valuable lesson, so openly discuss the story with your teacher, mentor, family, and friends. I also encourage you to feel free to send an e-mail to offer feedback, share pastry pictures, or just say hello! Here's my e-mail address: PrincessShayRead@aol.com.

With Lots of Love,
Princess Shay

Remember to "**Share, Eat, and Enjoy! SEE**, it always tastes better when we share."

P.S. There are discussion questions and other fun activities available at the end of the book.

Princess Shay

Let's Bake A Cake!

Step 1:
Make a list of all the tools and ingredients you do not already have in your kitchen required to bake a cake. Please ask a parent or adult family member to help! You will need his or her assistance in using all the equipment in the kitchen. Therefore, plan ahead and ask early.

Important Note: *If you or your family members have any type of food allergies, please substitute recipe ingredients as needed according to your physician.*

Tools:
Large Spoon
Small Spoon
2 Large Bowls
Measuring Cup
Measuring Spoons
Muffin/Cupcake Baking Pan
Cupcake Baking Cups
Ice Cream Scoop
Hand Mixer (optional)
Hand Towels
Oven
Apron

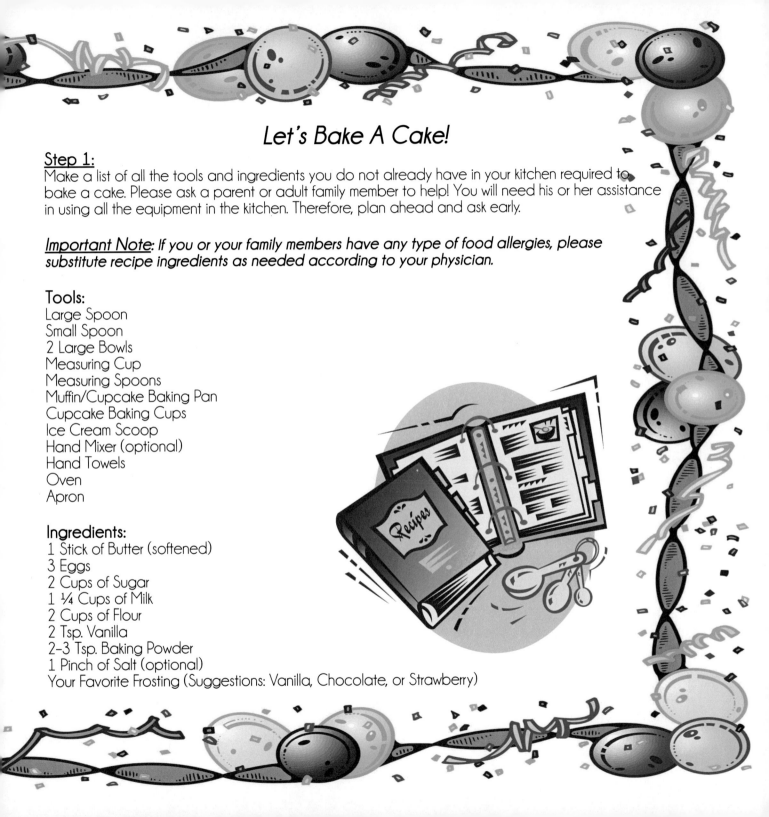

Ingredients:
1 Stick of Butter (softened)
3 Eggs
2 Cups of Sugar
1 ¼ Cups of Milk
2 Cups of Flour
2 Tsp. Vanilla
2-3 Tsp. Baking Powder
1 Pinch of Salt (optional)
Your Favorite Frosting (Suggestions: Vanilla, Chocolate, or Strawberry)

Step 2:

Now, let's put on our aprons, wash our hands, and get started! Wait, young prince and princess bakers, don't forget to ask for help. A parent or adult should be with you now to aid in the cooking process. Let the fun begin ... Adults will turn on the oven and preheat it to 350 degrees F. Then, using your measuring cup and spoons, measure your ingredients as needed so we can get mixing!

Step 3:

Take one of the large bowls, and add to it flour along with baking powder. Using the large spoon, blend these two ingredients together. Set aside. We will use this dry mixture later.

Step 4:

Take your second large bowl, and add to it butter, sugar, and salt (optional). Using the hand mixer or large spoon, mix these ingredients together for about 1 to 2 minutes. Next, add your vanilla and eggs one at a time until blended. Now, remember the mixture we set aside in Step 3? Let's add it a little at a time along with the milk until all the dry mixture has blended into a nice smooth batter.

Step 5:

Get your muffin or cupcake baking pan. Add the cupcake baking cups to each compartment in the pan. Using the ice cream scoop, dip into the batter from Step 4, and pour the mixture into each baking cup. Once all the cups have been filled, pick up the pan and softly drop it onto the counter.

Step 6:

Put the yummy cupcake batter into the preheated oven. Allow about 20 to 25 minutes for the baking process or until the cupcakes are done, because oven cooking times vary. Once complete, use the hand towels to aid in removing the very hot pan from the oven, but allow the adult to be the hero for this part of the baking step! Then, let the tasty treats cool for about 15 to 20 minutes.

Step 7:

Using the small spoon, scoop a mound of your favorite frosting onto the top of each cupcake and spread it to cover all the edges. Do I need to tell you what happens next?

Step 8:

"Share, Eat, and Enjoy! SEE, it always tastes better when we share." —Princess Shay

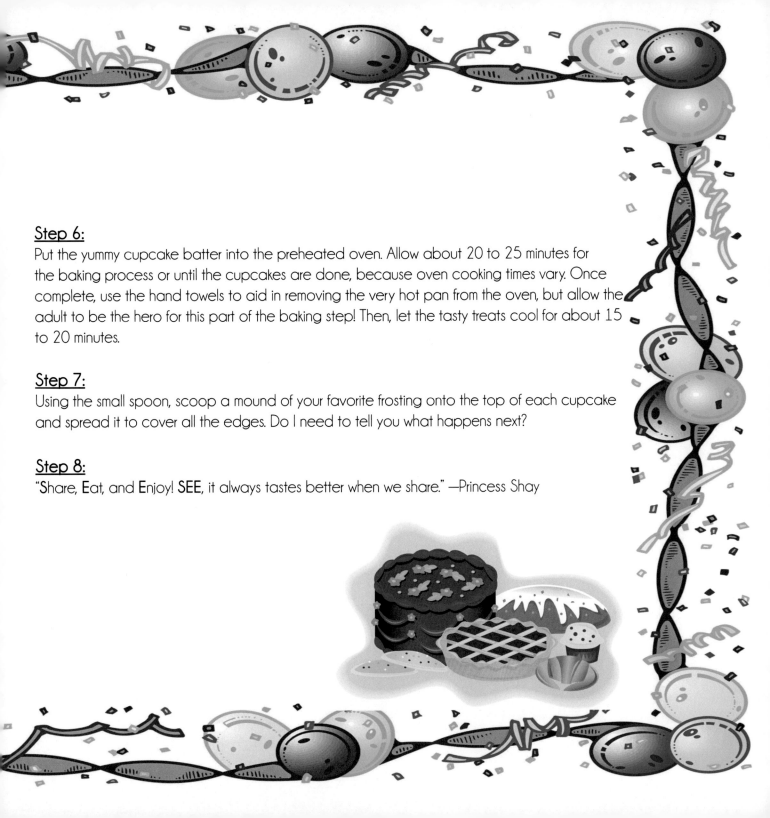

Everybody's Talking About...

Princess Shay's Good Manners Reminder

Always wash your hands before cooking and serving food.

Don't forget to clean up after the baking is finished.

Whenever we receive help, it is good manners to say thank you. I have created a special note for you to present to anyone who helped in the baking process or using the scissors.

With Lots of Love,

Princess Shay

THANK YOU!

World's Best

Dear _____
(Name)

Thank you for all of your help!

I am glad you were available to help me bake a cake.
We created a beautiful kitchen memory to cherish forever.

With Love,

_____
(Your Name)

cut here — cut here — cut here — cut here — cut here — cut here — cut here — cut here — cut here — cut here — cut here — cut here — cut here

Look for future books from Princess Shay

Feel free to send an e-mail to offer feedback, share pastry pictures, or just say hello!
E-mail: PrincessShayRead@aol.com

OR
Send a Royal Letter by postal carrier to the following:

P.O. Box 88001
Carol Stream, IL 60188
(For a Limited Time Only)

I look forward to hearing from you soon!

CONGRATULATIONS!
2010 Fiscal #1 IL District Wilton Method Instructor of Cake Decorating
Highest % Enrollment Increase Award
&
a proud supporter of the nonprofit organization
Great American Bake Sale
participant since 2007

To learn more, visit their Web site: www.strength.org.

Look for future books from Princess Shay

Feel free to send an e-mail to offer feedback, share pastry pictures, or just say hello!
E-mail: PrincessShayRead@aol.com

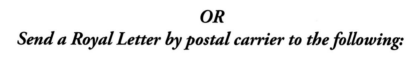

Send a Royal Letter by postal carrier to the following:

P.O. Box 88001
Carol Stream, IL 60188
(For a Limited Time Only)

I look forward to hearing from you soon!

CONGRATULATIONS!
2010 Fiscal #1 IL District Wilton Method Instructor of Cake Decorating
Highest % Enrollment Increase Award
&
a proud supporter of the nonprofit organization
Great American Bake Sale
participant since 2007

To learn more, visit their Web site: www.strength.org.

A Letter of Gratitude

I would like to thank my family for their constant encouragement to pursue my dreams and to believe that success is only a try away. I would also like to sincerely thank my aunt, Ophelia Carter-Boyd, for being our family pioneer in entrepreneurship and to commend her as a divinely talented abstract artist.

Most of all, I send a special thanks to all my friends that assisted in story review and editing, and thanks to my parents for saying, "Yes, you can…!"

Thank you to all my ancestors, and I humbly salute you as trailblazers.
Thank you for reserving a space for me!

Generations of Women Empowerment
Copyright 2003, OBoydDesigns
E-mail: Boydspirit@aol.com
All artwork contents are registered with the United States government.

FUN ACTIVITIES TO SHARE

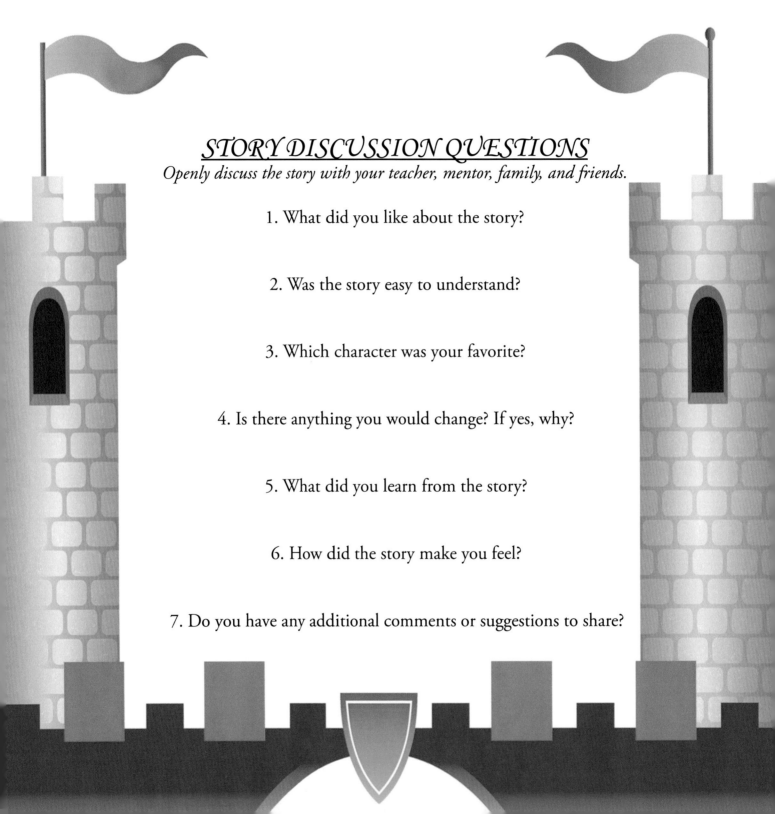

STORY DISCUSSION QUESTIONS

Openly discuss the story with your teacher, mentor, family, and friends.

1. What did you like about the story?

2. Was the story easy to understand?

3. Which character was your favorite?

4. Is there anything you would change? If yes, why?

5. What did you learn from the story?

6. How did the story make you feel?

7. Do you have any additional comments or suggestions to share?

ROYAL NOTES:

_____

_____

_____

_____

_____

_____

_____

_____

_____

_____

STORY CHARACTERS

Introducing the stars of the story in no particular order: Princess Shay, Measuring Spoon, Ms. Cake, Butter, Eggs, Sugar, Salt, Flour, and Vanilla

Cut out all the characters and pretend to mix the ingredients with Princess Shay in their appropriate order to bake a beautiful cake. Please don't forget to ask an adult for help using the scissors!

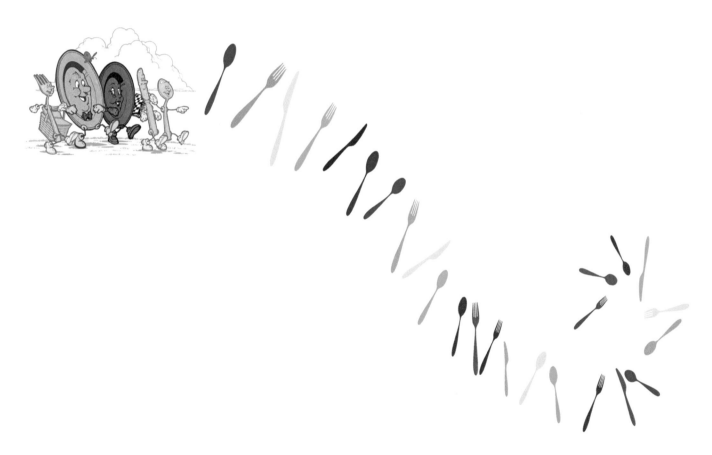

Remember, Princess Shay says, "**S**hare, **E**at, and **E**njoy! **SEE**, it always tastes better when we share."

Butter

Salt

Vanilla

Sugar

Princess Shay

Measuring Spoon

Flour

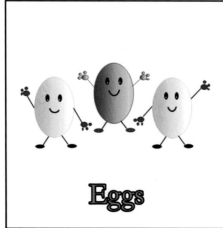

Eggs

Ms. Cake

Vanilla

Salt

Butter

Measuring Spoon

Princess Shay

Sugar

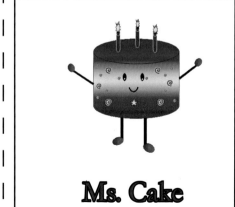

Ms. Cake

Eggs

Flour

WHAT'S ON YOUR CUPCAKE?

Color on It, Draw on It , Make It Beautiful!
A great cake starts with an idea.

EXERCISE YOUR BRAIN WITH THIS BAKING TEASER

*Can you help Princess Shay find all the
baking ingredients or cooking tools in the puzzle?*

R	U	O	L	F	P	M
B	U	T	R	K	A	I
B	O	W	L	O	N	L
S	U	G	A	V	M	K
E	G	G	S	E	I	C
S	P	O	O	N	L	A
V	A	N	I	L	L	A
B	S	U	G	A	R	J
D	B	U	T	T	E	R

Search for the following:

1. Spoon   6. Butter
2. Bowl   7. Eggs
3. Pan   8. Flour
4. Oven   9. Vanilla
5. Sugar   10. Milk

___Hint___: The words can be found up, down, horizontal, or backwards.
Check your answers on the next page.

EXERCISE YOUR BRAIN WITH THIS BAKING TEASER
Answers:

R	*U*	*O*	*L*	*E*	*P*	*M*
B	U	T	R	K	A	*I*
B	O	*W*	L	O	N	*L*
S	U	G	A	*V*	M	*K*
E	*G*	*G*	*S*	*E*	I	C
S	P	O	O	N	L	A
V	A	N	I	L	L	A
B	S	U	G	A	R	J
D	B	U	T	T	E	R

CAKE DECORATING IS FUN!

DID YOU KNOW YOU CAN…

TAKE A CLASS,
HAVE A PARTY,
HAVE A TEAM BUILDER EVENT,
& MORE ?
Available for kids & adults to learn cake decorating techniques

LOVE PRINCESS SHAY & BAKERY FRIENDS BOOK ?

DID YOU KNOW YOU CAN…

SCHEDULE A BOOK SIGNING,
LIVE READING,
OR COOKING PARTY?
Fun for all ages!

To learn more about the activities mentioned,
please send E-mail to the following:
LadyShayGourmet@aol.com

WEB SITE COMING SOON!

Everybody's Talking About...
Delicious Confessions

"Some of the best cooking I've ever had...."
-Jonathan O., Atlanta, GA

"Party felt like a once in a lifetime experience. Had an awesome time!"

-Robert W., Bloomingdale, IL

"An amazingly rich and smooth taste that lasts long after you've finished your slice!"

-Derwin D., Chicago, IL

"I've never tasted a chocolate cake so moist and chocolaty. The frosting was rich and creamy, not too sweet. Excellent!"

-Mary T., Crystal Lake, IL

"The party was excellent! Great food! Great music! Great everything! It was a lot of fun and everyone had a blast!"

-Jefferson B., Jackson, MS

"The cake made me feel like royalty!"

-Rashara G., St. Louis, MO

BONUS
COLORING PAGES

Have fun Princes & Princesses!
With Lots of Love,
Princess Shay

Remember to "Share, Eat, and Enjoy! **SEE**, it always tastes better when we share."

Butter

Vanilla

Flour

Eggs

Salt

Sugar

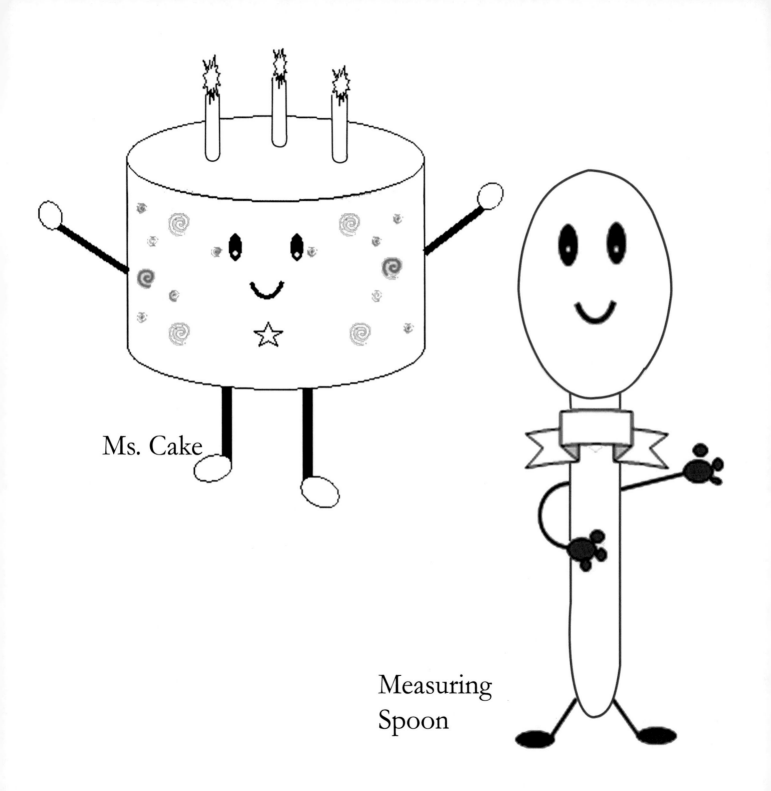

Ms. Cake

Measuring
Spoon

Princess Shay & Bakery Friends

Make A New Discovery!

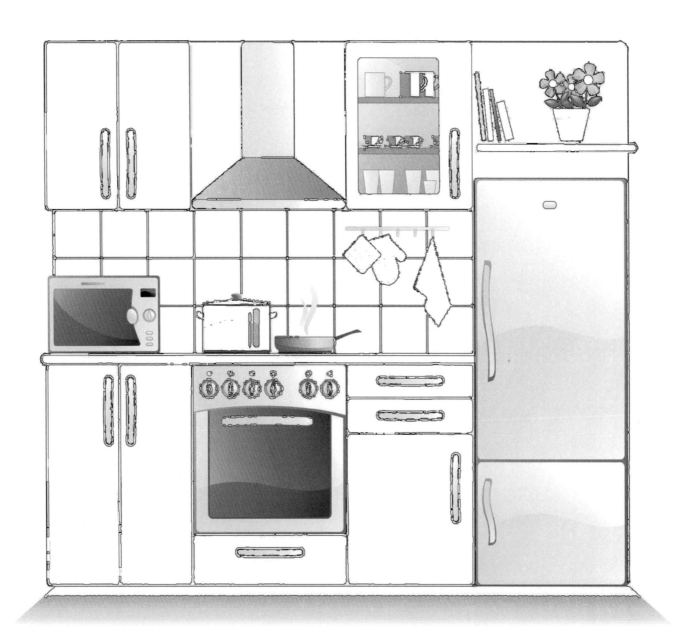

Baked Goodies & Cake Gallery Photos

Food Journal

Exercise Journal

Are you exercising? Write down your goals.

_____

_____

_____

_____

_____

_____

_____

_____

_____

Keep Moooooving! Milk is good, but don't forget to drink water.

		1	2	3	4
5	6	7	8	9	10
11	12	13	14	15	16
17	18	19	20	21	22
23	24	25	26	27	28
29	30	31			

Shopping List

1. _____
2. _____
3. _____
4. _____
5. _____
6. _____
7. _____
8. _____
9. _____
10. _____

11. _____
12. _____
13. _____
14. _____
15. _____
16. _____
17. _____
18. _____
19. _____
20. _____

21. _____
22. _____
23. _____
24. _____
25. _____
26. _____
27. _____
28. _____
29. _____
30. _____

The Royal Contact List

Date	Name	Comments
____	_____	_____
____	_____	_____
____	_____	_____
____	_____	_____
____	_____	_____
____	_____	_____
____	_____	_____
____	_____	_____
____	_____	_____
____	_____	_____

Book Signing Party!

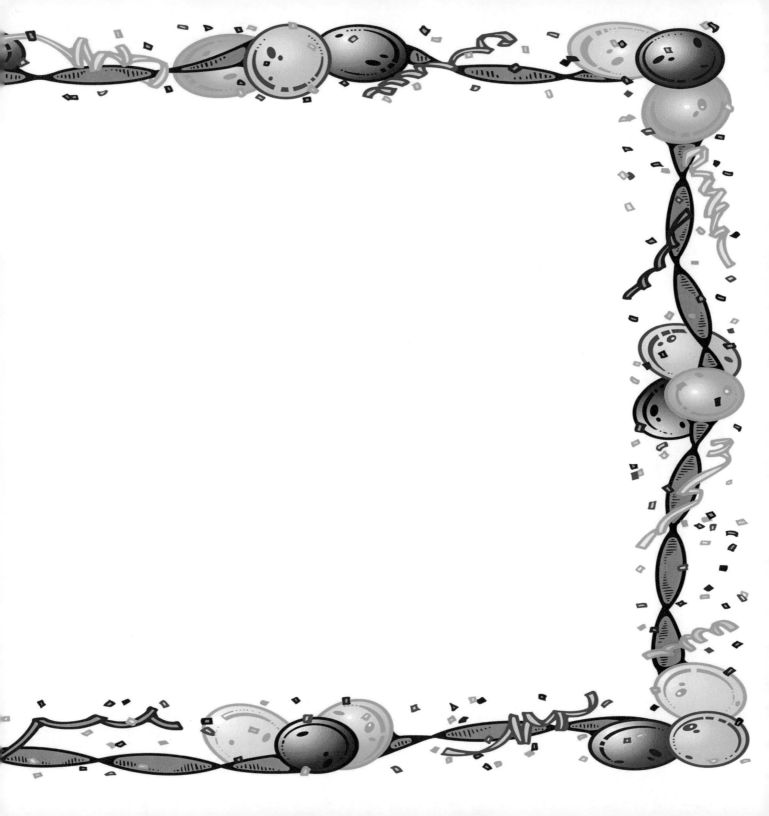

Everybody's Talking About...

**Princess Shay & Bakery Friends
Make a New Discovery!**

About the Author

Shalonda Carter, an accomplished honors graduate of Jackson State University and computer science professional, has a passion for food and social entertaining. As a result, she branches into a different world of "bits and bytes" as a culinary artist. Her unique sense of creativity and extraordinary talent led to her induction into the Wilton Century Club in 2009 for having provided pastry decorating instruction to more than one hundred students. Shalonda also recently earned the 2010 Fiscal #1 Illinois District Wilton Method Instructor of Cake Decorating Highest Percentage Enrollment Award in recognition of her contributions to increased student enrollment for Wilton course instruction, and she is a certified professional wedding and event planner.

Using her corporate and culinary experiences as a foundation, Shalonda strives to teach children and remind adults of important life lessons in her writing. She also hopes this first book will inspire families to begin creating fond memories of cooking in their kitchens, memories similar to those of her cooking with family and especially her grandmother. All in all, Shalonda believes learning is a continuous process of life, and "Success is only a try away to endless possibilities!"

A Personal Testimonial

"A skilled craft of patience that is appealing to the eyes, intriguing for the senses, and nearly overwhelming per the attention to delightful details. . . That is the artistic experience of the cake and the event I strive to create!"

–Shalonda Carter "Shay"

Thank you to the Oprah show for its entrepreneurial television program featuring Warren Brown from CakeLove. This show motivated me to educate myself on business start-ups and has helped me to arrive at this pivotal moment in my life.

Thank you, Warren, for being an inspiration and for your words of encouragement!

Overall, I would also like to thank all of my friends and students for your support. Thank you for enriching my life by sharing your love for pastry decorating and your sweet tooth!

Printed in the United States
By Bookmasters